A
HANDBOOK
FOR THOSE
WORKING WITH
THE ELDERLY

THINKING IT THROUGH

To St Mary's Launceston and Lee Mill Hospitals who were the inspiration, and to Torquil for his encouragement.

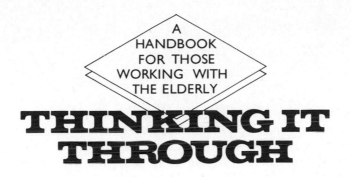

A HANDBOOK FOR THOSE WORKING WITH THE ELDERLY

THINKING IT THROUGH

UNA P HOLDEN

ILLUSTRATED BY JEAN DE LEMOS

WP

WINSLOW PRESS

9, London Lane, London E8 3PR Telephone: 01-533 0315

Una P Holden qualified as a Clinical Psychologist in Liverpool and worked in Lancashire before spending some years in the United States at the Missouri Institute of Psychiatry. From 1975 her work at St James's University Hospital, Leeds, led to developments in services to the elderly and in the field of neuropsychology. She has presented papers and published in this country and abroad.

Until recently Una Holden was Principal Clinical Psychologist, Plymouth Health District, and Chief Clinical Tutor, MSc Clinical Psychology, at Plymouth Polytechnic. At present she provides a regular service to Somerset Health Services and she also runs training courses at several universities and polytechnics throughout the country.

First published in 1984 by
Winslow Press, Telford Road, Bicester, Oxon OX6 0TS
Reprinted 1986, 1988
Copyright © Una P Holden, 1984
Illustrations © Winslow Press, 1984
ISBN 0 86388 015 0

02 0146
Printed in Great Britain by
Hobbs the Printers, Southampton

CONTENTS

1

Normal Ageing

INTELLIGENCE, PERSONALITY AND ENVIRONMENT

Despite all common belief, to be elderly does not mean that intellectual decline is inevitable. The elderly are not headed for the 'cabbage patch'. Studies and investigations have shown that the majority of the elderly:

■ can learn
■ have good coping skills
■ can solve problems
■ retain and use abilities and skills
■ verbalise better than younger people, though they may take longer to do so – they think more cautiously and consider various possibilities
■ have an intellectual level which is as varied as any other age group – because of this, it is highly probable that as individuals they are much brighter than many younger people
■ have memories which are as good or as faulty as those of younger people.

A teenager is called scatterbrained when a phone message is forgotten, an older person is called 'senile' ... We all suffer from Benign Forgetfulness!

Long-term memory in older people is generally quite good. Short-term memory may require some help. In schools and colleges the memorising of information is aided by the use of video, film, tapes and other forms of sensory input. The

elderly person is expected to remember after being *told* something only once. To underestimate the ability of an older person is not justified.

Illness, problems and pressures can influence most people. Generally there is no proof of basic changes in personality over the years, unless there is a specific reason. The old saying 'To be a sweet old lady it is necessary to be a sweet young one' is worth remembering... The converse can be true too!

Older people are as much a product of their environment as anyone else. The habits, pastimes and beliefs of a community are well ingrained, so factors of major importance include:

- education
- social achievement or 'standing'
- social standards or mores
- living in town or country
- finance
- family relationships
- group membership
- hobbies and interests
- occupations.

All play a major role in the life of an individual. They help to shape personality, affect the daily lives of people and also influence their expectations. Age does not change these attitudes, needs or expectations, but those of the community or its individual members can. So if the belief of a culture/community is that age implies something unpleasant, elderly people may well believe this themselves. This could account for the so-called 'lack of motivation' often seen.

There are approximately 60 million people in Great Britain and of these about 8,000,000 are classed as elderly. 10% of this latter population is the commonly accepted figure for

the number of elderly in need of some form of care. Statistics concerning this group are the ones most frequently quoted. Such emphasis totally misrepresents the vast majority of fit, well and independent elderly who continue with their lives unnoticed. As we work with the sick, infirm and the confused it is only too easy to forget what normal elderly people are like ... or even that they exist at all.

BASIC NEEDS OF THE ELDERLY

The basic needs of the elderly, whether they are normal, physically disabled or mentally infirm, are more or less the same as those of everyone else. They include:

- financial security
- emotional security
- recognition of individuality
- choice in decision making
- being treated as a whole person
- good health
- good relationships
- adequate nutrition
- a home of their own choice in an environment of their own choosing
- group membership, to provide an outlet for skills, interests and support
- privacy, both personal and in a limited group such as the family.

—2—
Communication

We all communicate both verbally and non-verbally (body language).

Verbal

We can run into problems with people from other parts of the country. On visiting another country which speaks our language we can still have strange experiences owing to differences in the use of language. The use of stress on different syllables can change the meaning of a word or sentence, e.g. how many ways can you say the word 'Great' and imply something totally different?

Non-verbal

Every family, every couple has secret languages. A smile, a shrug, a gesture can have a very personal meaning. Groups, people from different parts of the country, or from different cultures can all imply different things by the use of the same gesture. We take most of this for granted and expect elderly people to pick up our meaning. We forget some basic facts:

i   Body movements may be difficult. Gestures may be cut to a minimum with age. Parkinson's Disease, for instance, can cause a face to look fixed and expression-less so that the person appears unfriendly. In fact, they are just incapable of expression.

ii Eyesight may be poor and a gesture by a younger person may be too far away, or may have come into use too recently to be meaningful.

iii It is harder for an old person to move into or away from a conversation. Particular aspects of communication should be considered:

Speech defects

These can be due to physical disability such as cleft palate, or to actual illness such as stroke, fever or delirium, or to mental disturbances. Aphasia (difficulty with speech) does not imply total intellectual damage: not being able to speak does not mean not being able to think. People can still express themselves in some way. So when a person has problems in understanding try:

- speaking slowly, clearly and using a short sentence;
- asking one question instead of offering alternatives, e.g. 'Would you like coffee?' instead of 'Would you like coffee or tea?'

Make sure that patients use false teeth that fit, wear properly prescribed glasses and use a working hearing aid. Even those entering hospital or home without aids may in fact require them.

Sensory acuity

There is a loss of sensory acuity in normal ageing. So in order to establish good communication this has to be taken into account. It is helpful to:

- speak to individuals, not to the room/ward as a whole;
- get near to a person, preferably to the front and side, or, even better, at eye level;
- use touch to attract attention, to help people concentrate and to express gentle concern and understanding;
- avoid approaching someone from behind as this can be perceived as a threat and can startle;
- hold attention by using visual, auditory, olfactory or tactile stimuli: in other words provide relevant pictures, materials to touch and feel, things to listen to or to smell;

- increase attention span and memory by repetition of the content of the conversation, rather than by parrot-like and uninspiring repetition of the same words;

- remember senses such as taste, touch and smell which are often forgotten: loss of these senses is quite common and could explain many behaviours or statements, e.g. 'This tastes poisonous!'

EXERCISES

Aspects to consider during exercises and conversation with very confused people:

1 What sort of language is employed today that is different from twenty or thirty years ago?

2 Do you always understand your children's or teenagers' language?

3 Have you ever had problems getting a foreigner to understand your English or your use of 'expressions'?

4 If you had lost your ability to:
   (a) hear
   (b) see
   (c) touch
   (d) taste
   (e) smell
   (f) speak
   how do you think you would manage? What difference would it make?

5 Do you know people who are unable to speak properly? What do you think of them? What do you think they can do?

6 What about body language, or non-verbal communication? Do you think you use it?

7 What sort of gestures do you use with your family that no one else knows about?

ROLE PLAY IDEAS

1 (a) How do you think a young person could attract the attention of an interesting member of the opposite sex without using words?

(b) Try role play of making a shy person use eye contact.

2 What sort of gestures are used in this country that are meaningful to everyone?

3 Use bandages, ear plugs and rubber gloves on several members of staff in a training session, so that they can experience what sensory deprivation is really like.

4 (a) What gestures can be encouraging?

(b) What gestures can be alarming or threatening?

5 How do you feel about touching someone or being touched by someone?

6 What would happen if a person's face was only twelve inches away from yours? What could happen between two people face to face at that distance?

7 At what distance should a group sit from each other to make conversation (a) possible, (b) impossible?

8 How can a situation be avoided without using words, e.g. avoiding an objectionable stranger/acquaintance?

9 How can you ensure that no one intrudes on your chosen patch?

10 Do you think that other cultures/countries use non-verbal communication? What for instance?

11 If you were on your own in a strange environment what would you look for which would communicate different kinds of information to you?

12 Do you feel everyone needs a 'sacred' area of personal space, i.e. six inches past the nose?

13 If you were unable to move, would this affect your ability to converse? If so, how?

DISCUSSION TOPICS

1   Surely talking about day, date, weather and name is patronising?

2   How can you talk to someone who is rambling and talking nonsense?

3   Someone with speech problems is unable to understand, or join in a conversation.

4   What is the point of introducing things to taste, touch, smell and see to a confused person?

5   Why cannot we call an old person by his/her first name without permission?

3
Stimulation

We all need colour to express our personality. We decorate our home to suit our tastes, gather souvenirs and things that interest *us*. We organise our home to suit our needs and know exactly where everything is kept or placed.

Hospitalisation and residential care can deprive us of this familiarity and self-organisation. This can, so very quickly, cause institutionalisation as it becomes necessary to rely on others for general orientation.

Stimulation must be meaningful: radios and televisions that are outside control produce adverse effects rather like 'brain washing'. It is a fact that being unable to have some control over one's life leads to feelings of hopelessness. The effects of such lack of control were much in evidence in prisoner-of-war camps during World War II.

To 'sit and be good' may be helpful to staff wanting to get on with their duties, but to patients and residents it is an invitation to vegetate. Activities, responsibilities, self-care, however simple, and the pursuit of skills must all be considered in order to encourage residents and patients to continue to have some say in their style of existence.

Patients and residents need stimulation as much as anyone else. Physical care is not enough: mental stimulation is *vital* to normal living.

POSSIBLE CHANGES

1 Only use television or radio when people want it, or when someone can discuss what is happening.

2 Provide seasonal fruit and flowers that can be seen, touched and smelled.

3 Create an atmosphere, a simulated pub, normal living room, library area.

4 Organise outings, parties, competitions.

5 Grow plants, have an indoor aviary, organise the making of toys to give to children in a home.

6 Ensure newspapers are available.

7 Encourage people to look after themselves and each other.

DISCUSSION TOPICS

1 Why should the elderly be interested in current events?

2 Why is the past of use in conversation between younger and older people?

3 Why should seasonal fruit and flowers be useful?

4 Why should television and radio not be on all the time? Surely it gives clients something to do?

5 What effect does uncontrolled noise have? What effect does lack of control over the environment have?

4

Environment

As noted above, colour and personal possessions are of immense importance to us. We *choose* our homes, what we put in them, and who we entertain therein. Our environment has special stimulating features for us. It provides us with our private place and it permits us to share this space with those close to us. It is familiar, well learned, understood and comfortable. It does not threaten.

A bad or lacking environment can produce adverse effects. It can cause withdrawal. Circumstances which may cause a bad environment include:

- lack of money
- lack of transport
- failing mobility, sensory loss, stroke
- frailty
- bereavement/loss of family
- poor nutrition
- lack of opportunity to pursue interests and social outlets.

The effects of any of these could be enough to provoke gloomy thoughts in any age group. Old people often respond by becoming depressed, or by withdrawing. Far too frequently this is interpreted as 'dementia'.

EXERCISES

Individuals or staff groups could consider the following:

1 How is your home organised to suit you?
Where are your knives and forks?
Where is your best china?
What sort of things do you keep in a special place?
Can you always find what you want?
Do you have special cupboards for dry goods/tinned goods?
Do you have books in a special place and order?
2 How do you find your way home?
3 Why did you choose where you live?
4 What is it about your home that made you choose it?
5 When you furnished it, why did you make changes to the way it was before you arrived?
6 Are there certain colours you could not live with?
7 When you last moved home what difficulties did you experience in organising your new home?
8 Who are the people who spend most time in your home?
9 Are you a member of many groups?
10 Are there special things you keep for your family, or belonging to them?

It is the business of the 'caring professions' to modify the institutionalising environments. The following factors should be considered.

LOOKING AT THE PHYSICAL ENVIRONMENT

Check whether the following are available, or could be improved:

- Public space.
- Private space.
- Toilets easy to find and offering privacy.

- Daily living areas.
- Accessible amenities.
- Clothes washing facilities for clients.
- Simple kitchen for clients.
- Lighting – it is clear, bright enough and not causing illusions?
- Steps – how many are there, and can they be easily managed?
- Do long corridors have directions, arrows, lines on the floor or walls?
- Mirrors, bright atmosphere and colour.
- Table and chair groupings for easy conversation.
- Light coloured walls and ceilings.
- Safe floors (which look safe too).
- Tea and snack making facilities.
- Cupboards with games and home crafts easy to find.
- Sewing machines, tools, bar, games table.
- Good view.
- Outdoor facilities – for sitting and for activities.
- Opportunities and facilities for reminiscence.

Decor and information (cues)

Are the following ideas/aids in use?

Toilets: are the doors easy for men and women to identify? They can be made easy to find by using:

    a different colour from other doors;

    a special pattern;

    Contact/Fablon;

    stripes;

    left-over piece of interesting wallpaper;

    arrows/lines on wall or floor;

    a full-length outline of a man/woman.

Colour coding: for rooms, doors, private areas, etc.

Personal possessions on view: for identification, orientation, pleasure and self-esteem.

Notice boards etc: for current information. It is useful to have:

> notice boards in a central place providing information about events;
>
> large, clear calendars with basic information on day, date, place and weather;
>
> a large, clear clock;
>
> fruit, flowers and seasonal pictures and objects;
>
> a menu for the day and perhaps the next day;
>
> newspapers and magazines.

Directions: in colour, pictures and large words. Orientation and independence can be increased by simple additions to the decor. These could include:

> the presence of useful signs which have pictures as well as words, e.g. Dining Room in large letters and on a picture of people eating;
>
> rooms with occupier's name and photograph;
>
> large notice with everyone's name and photograph, including staff;
>
> use of personal possessions to aid identification of private space (this also helps a person to feel at home);
>
> colour coding generally – private and public areas, beds, toilets, etc.;
>
> cupboards with pictures and words to identify contents.

5

Psychological Environment

Interaction

Do staff talk to clients?

Do staff use the cues in the surroundings?

Do staff use RO type methods of providing information? (see pp.37 and 41.)

Do the clients talk to each other?

Are there any facilities to encourage interaction?

Are recreational facilities available?

General understanding of psychological aspects

Do all the staff understand enough about:

- normal ageing;
- basic communication skills;
- the needs of the elderly;
- the abilities of the clients;
- the background of the clients;
- the need for a group identity;
- sensory deprivation;
- the implications of 'confusion';
- the implications of specific 'brain damage' such as aphasia?

EXERCISES AND DISCUSSION TOPICS

Try filling in the Orientation Facilities Checklist (see Appendix, page 41). Are these things available, or could they be improved?

Discuss the implications of the following:

1 Why should correct lighting be important?
2 How does this relate to visual acuity and the elderly?
3 Can lighting cause strange illusions? If so, what effect could these have on behaviour and our interpretation of observed behaviour?
4 Why is public and private space important?
5 What value is there to clients in having notices, directions and colour coding? What is the point of having pictures as well as words?
6 What is the relationship between the environment and stimulation?

Groups

Membership of a group is a basic human need. We belong to a group from the day we are born. The family provides the 'ground rules' and teaches us about the tools that we will need to cope with life.

As we grow we become involved with other groups which influence our beliefs, responses, behaviour and self-evaluation. Such groups include our street and neighbours, school, work, interests, and friends. More distant, impersonal or general group influences like nationality, religion, race, politics, even our sex, can affect us.

Groups teach us, guide us and provide rules and sanctions. In our need for other people, or for outlets for our interests and personality, we will modify our behaviour to comply with the needs of the group, or groups, to which we belong.

Children need group membership and influence, and so do adults. The elderly are also adults and they too need group membership and identity. Without the support of a group the elderly become vulnerable. Confusion and withdrawal can result.

To be outside a recognised group, and possibly subject to its influence, and to be aware of a lack of control over the situation can be a terrifying experience for the isolated individual of any age.

Individuals must have something in common for a group to form. Elderly, confused people removed from their home are too disturbed by the event to use normal social skills in order to make contact with others. A 'guide' or 'leader', who is a member of staff or a very alert resident, is required.

GROUP COMMITMENT

This is necessary for the survival of any group, but it can be dangerous if the *reason* for the group is forgotten i.e. care staff groups arise due to the need to provide service for the customer (patient/resident). If the only group is staff based then the elderly are disadvantaged and deprived. To avoid danger to the client, staff must ensure that:

■ They understand their own group.

■ They play their individual role in helping it to succeed.

■ They are aware that commitment to a staff group alone could be damaging to the needs of the client.

■ They realise the ability of staff groups to influence those in their care for good or bad.

■ They remember that the staff group is responsible for the development of group awareness in clients by:

(a) preserving the individual;

(b) providing interaction so the individual remains a human being;

(c) providing opportunities for the development of a client group;

(d) providing the necessary support to maintain the client group.

RO and Group Living Concepts are two possible ways of achieving and satisfying this group need.

7

Confusion

There is confusion about the word 'confusion'! What does it mean? What, if anything, can be done about it?

When a child has a fever or a temperature everyone accepts that he or she can ramble, can say or do silly things. Everyone accepts that this is due to illness. Usually when someone over the age of sixty behaves in the same way the observer assumes that it is due to something called 'Senile Dementia'. How many people ever consider fever, or the fact that we all suffer from 'Benign Forgetfulness'? Illness causes confusion. Treatment of illness should restore rational thought and behaviour.

Rather than jumping to unfounded and dire conclusions a proper investigation should be made. The person's life style might reveal poor nutrition, poor home conditions and intense isolation... all possible causes of *delirium*. Various mental disorders, depression for example, can prove to be the cause. Incorrectly used medication, heart disease and other purely medical problems, vitamin deficiency, neurological states, social upsets and many, many other factors could be responsible for the person's condition.

The various dementia-related states – Alzheimer's (senile dementia), and some more rare disease processes – are usually seen as total failure of brain function. This is simply not the case. The person who is totally demented is really very rare. Most people are severely withdrawn and suffer from specific impairments rather than being completely incapable.

It is vital to find a *positive* aspect in all people, whether deteriorated or not. There are many things that so-called 'demented' people can still do. In the first place, look at each person for the *good* aspects of their function or behaviour. It is a good idea to start at the beginning: can he or she even breathe? Can they move? What can they do for themselves? Slowly a picture of a *person* can be built up and this will provide a base on which to build. Retained abilities can be used, and damaged abilities may improve, or others may adapt.

PRACTICAL APPROACHES TO CONFUSED BEHAVIOUR

First of all spend some time *observing* the person. At different times of the day and according to different situations, behaviour can change.

Make sure that the confusion is not physically or emotionally based.

Decide how to help.

If certain abilities/behaviours need to be changed or improved, **set simple targets**, e.g.:

■ Design a stage by stage method to learn the way to the toilet.

■ Find ways to repeat, encourage associations, use visual cues, in order to learn the name of a member of staff or another patient/resident.

■ Use similar ways to help the remembering of, for example, the name of the home or ward.

Each target will need to be broken down into stages. Each stage must allow for specific problems . . . it would be silly to provide written material for someone who cannot read.

Retained ability can be used as much as possible, e.g. recognition of pictures or drawings. The person may not speak but can understand pictures, so a set of pictures on

'How to make a sandwich' would be helpful. Be prepared to spend some time on the 'teaching' process.

Think through the way before starting. He or she may be able to learn better with reading material, by being shown how to do something, or by seeing pictures or drawings of the actions required.

Try to get other staff or patients to help. It is essential that everyone uses the same approach.

Keep a note of progress and time spent.

Make sure to use praise for every little success.

When one thing is learned go on to the next.

Do not forget to keep the targets low and within the probability of success.

Do not bore someone by delaying the next step too long.

Record success. Everyone should know about any success.

8

Reality Orientation

There are many papers and books to consult about this approach. Here Reality Orientation (RO) will only be considered in the light of a twenty-four hour approach and the implications of RO and the environment.

1   At first a very confused person may not be able to respond to the environment. The sooner a person can be made aware of environmental cues and the available amenities the better. So a reasonably aware person should be guided around on arrival.

2   Simple measures are the best with the very confused. They need special treatment to encourage them and to give them renewed confidence.
(a) Use simple day, date and weather information.
(b) Draw their attention to activities and things happening around them.
(c) Warmth, repetition and interest will help.
(d) Gently find out about their interests, abilities and experience and use these in conversation.
(e) Point out the environmental cues at every opportunity.
(f) Look for positive aspects.

3   As soon as possible help people to form a social group.

4   Find ways to encourage interaction.

5 Even very confused people can respond to things they can taste, touch and smell, as well as see.

6 Interaction will not occur unless there is some appreciation of how to group furniture to aid communication. It is also necessary to have things to do and to discuss.

7 Sometimes institution rules make it hard for residents/patients to live a normal existence. The resident/patient should come first and the rules could be modified to facilitate this.

8 A more 'advanced' group of clients could organise things for themselves and actually help the less able.

9 Retraining can be aided by the consistent use of cues in the environment. If this environment is planned correctly it can provide opportunities for people to continue to use simple daily living skills and so improve their independence.

DISCUSSION TOPICS

1 Think of ways to help an old person remember their way around. (Does someone act as a guide during the first few days?)

2 In what ways can the environment in your ward/home be used to encourage independence?

3 What would make *you* feel more 'at home' in your ward/home?

4 What can be done in your ward/home to help the elderly to:
■ remember
■ gain confidence
■ become orientated
■ use their abilities
■ use their skills
■ develop their interests?

5 What do you know about the past of the people in your care?

6 Are there any materials, objects, books or things which might prove particularly stimulating to the people in your care? What about their previous jobs?

7 What 'rules' could be changed or modified to meet the clients' needs?

■ Could they pour their own tea, or even make it when they want to?

■ Could they stay in bed a bit later and get a simple breakfast?

■ Could they stay up late to watch something special on television?

■ Could they hear the sort of music they like – opera, classical – without disturbing anyone else?

■ Could they serve their own meals, make their own beds. . . ?

—————APPENDIX—————

ORIENTATION FACILITIES (ORIF) CHECKLIST

This checklist was developed to assess facilities available to elderly persons living in hospitals and residential homes for the elderly. The first section assesses the available Orientation Facilities in relation to the physical environment. The second section helps to estimate the availability of sensory stimulation. The scoring system provides one choice in four for each question.

Rating scale:

Yes	Mainly	Rarely	No
1	2	3	4

Yes   In all categories. The facilities are available for all residents and in easy access.

Mainly Indicates that the facility is available, but not for all residents or not easily available.

Rarely Indicates that some attempt has been made at providing the facility, or that hardly anyone is able to utilise it.

No   Indicates that the facility is not offered at all.

Scoring key

I Architecture/environment

20 — 30 = A
31 — 40 = B
41 — 50 = C
51 — 60 = D

II Sensory stimulation

$20 - 30 = A$

$31 - 40 = B$

$41 - 50 = C$

$51 - 60 = D$

The scoring key enables a combined assessment score to be made. Some physical environments for instance may not be so pleasant because of their age, but may provide more sensory stimulation.

Orientation Facilities

$40 - 60 = A$

$61 - 80 = B$

$81 - 100 = C$

$101 - 120 = D$

The four categories are defined as follows:

A Positive environment

B Can be improved

C Orientation Facilities less than adequate

D Unstimulating, negative environment

I ARCHITECTURE/ENVIRONMENT

YES MAINLY RARELY NO

1 Are there signs (both verbal and pictorial) to indicate rooms (lounge, dining room etc.)? ☐ ☐ ☐ ☐

2 Are bedrooms easy to identify (colour coding, large nameplates, etc.)? ☐ ☐ ☐ ☐

3 Are toilet doors easy to identify for both men and women (colour, pattern, floor-markings on long corridors)? ☐ ☐ ☐ ☐

4 Is there a centrally placed notice board with basic information (day, month, weather, events of the day, place)? ☐ ☐ ☐ ☐

5 Are personal possessions on display in bedrooms to aid identification and independence? ☐ ☐ ☐ ☐

6 Are there facilities available for residents to make their own tea/toast? ☐ ☐ ☐ ☐

7 Is there a simple kitchen for residents? ☐ ☐ ☐ ☐

8 Can residents use their own laundry room? ☐ ☐ ☐ ☐

9 Are the chairs away from the walls? ☐ ☐ ☐ ☐

10 Are there several small tables around which a group of chairs are set? ☐ ☐ ☐ ☐

11 Is there a recreational area? ☐ ☐ ☐ ☐

12 Is there a quiet, private area? ☐ ☐ ☐ ☐

13 Are lounges in the centre of activity? ☐ ☐ ☐ ☐

14 Is the main staff office near the centre of activity? ☐ ☐ ☐ ☐

15 Does the Group Living Concept operate in the home? ☐ ☐ ☐ ☐

YES MAINLY RARELY NO

16 Are there any small rooms suitable for DIY use by four to five residents? ☐ ☐ ☐ ☐
If yes, do they have:

(a) a sink ☐ ☐ ☐ ☐

(b) sufficient electricity output for television /radio/reading lights ☐ ☐ ☐ ☐

(c) furnishing/equipment to allow for separate meals or activities? ☐ ☐ ☐ ☐

17 Is there a bar or an area where private drinking can take place? ☐ ☐ ☐ ☐

18 Is the lighting correct and appropriately placed? ☐ ☐ ☐ ☐

19 Are the floor areas seen as being safe by residents: they do not look slippery or uneven? ☐ ☐ ☐ ☐

20 Are specially adapted aids available (cutlery, tools, bathroom supports, kitchen gadgets)? ☐ ☐ ☐ ☐

II SENSORY STIMULATION

YES MAINLY RARELY NO

1 Is there a good view from windows? ☐ ☐ ☐ ☐

2 Do clients appear to control the use of television? ☐ ☐ ☐ ☐

3 Do clients appear to control playing of music? ☐ ☐ ☐ ☐

4 Are the decorations bright and cheerful? ☐ ☐ ☐ ☐

5 Are bedrooms bright, cheerful and personal? ☐ ☐ ☐ ☐

6 Are there newspapers readily available? ☐ ☐ ☐ ☐

7 Are there flowers and/or plants in every living room? ☐ ☐ ☐ ☐

8 Is fresh fruit easily available? ☐ ☐ ☐ ☐

9 Is there a selection of games or crafts readily available? ☐ ☐ ☐ ☐

10 Is there a library? ☐ ☐ ☐ ☐

11 Are there regular entertainment events? ☐ ☐ ☐ ☐

12 Are there daily opportunities for activity? ☐ ☐ ☐ ☐

13 Is there a choice of what occurs? ☐ ☐ ☐ ☐

14 Are residents informed of the events to take place? ☐ ☐ ☐ ☐

15 Are there books, pictures, etc., to aid reminiscence? ☐ ☐ ☐ ☐

16 Are there visits or outings to keep in touch with change and current events? ☐ ☐ ☐ ☐

17 Are there any games and pastimes to aid memory and spatial relationships? ☐ ☐ ☐ ☐

18 Is there any outside involvement with the community? YES MAINLY RARELY NO ☐ ☐ ☐ ☐

19 Can individuals control room temperature? ☐ ☐ ☐ ☐

20 Are clients reasonably occupied for most of the time, i.e. not left just sitting for hours on end? ☐ ☐ ☐ ☐

—FURTHER READING—

BOOKS

Rimmer, L, *Reality Orientation – Principles & Practice*, Winslow Press (1982).

Holden, U P and Woods, R T, *Reality Orientation*, Churchill Livingstone (1982).

Holden, U P, Martin, C and White M, *24 Hour Approach to the Problems of Confusion in Elderly People* (1980), published by Winslow Press (1984).

Rush, J and McCausland, T, *Working with 'Confused' Elderly People*, Kings Fund Centre, London (1982).

SLIDE-TAPE PROGRAMMES

Woods, R T, *Reality Orientation (1 and 2)* Graves Medical Audiovisual Library, Chelmsford, Essex.

Age Concern, *Recall*, series of 'reminiscence' tapes and slides.

Videos also available via author.

ACKNOWLEDGMENT

The Orientation Facilities Checklist was compiled with the assistance of Karen Ehlert.

Other publications by the same author of interest to those working with the elderly

R O Reminders

Pocket reference of ideas

Una Holden

An object may be made available to an R O Group, but ideas on its use do not come readily to mind. This handy pocket-sized booklet provides a quick reference when ideas run dry.

24 Hour Approach to the Problems of Confusion in Elderly People

Una Holden, Carol Martin and Margaret White

This booklet gives an outline of the general principles involved in the daily care of the elderly person.

Nostalgia

Series Editor – Una Holden

These reminiscence aids are a series of stimulus cards designed to encourage reflections and recollections of the past through objects, situations and events. Notes are provided in each case to encourage conversation.

Then & Now – Vehicles

40 photographs showing old and new vehicles.

Banner Headlines

30 cards showing banner headlines relating to major events that occurred during the period 1910–1950.

Royalty

30 cards showing different members of the Royal Family and royal events from 1910–1950.

Send for a catalogue to:

Winslow Press
Telford Road, Bicester, Oxon OX6 0TS